Extreme Sports

BMX

MATT DOEDEN

BLACK RABBIT BOOKS

Bolt is published by Black Rabbit Books
P.O. Box 227, Mankato, Minnesota, 56002
www.blackrabbitbooks.com

Alissa Thielges, editor; Michael Sellner, designer and photo researcher

Library of Congress Cataloging-in-Publication Data
Names: Doeden, Matt, author.
Title: BMX / Matt Doeden.
Description: Mankato, Minnesota: Black Rabbit Books, [2024] | Series: Extreme sports | Includes bibliographical references and index. | Audience: Ages 8-12 | Audience: Grades 4-6 | Summary: "Get your heart pumping with BMX, an extreme bike racing sport. Struggling and reluctant readers will discover the skills and equipment needed to race and compete in freestyle. Includes a table of contents, glossary with pronunciations, further resources, and an index"—Provided by publisher.
Identifiers: LCCN 2023008873 (print) | LCCN 2023008874 (ebook) | ISBN 9781623108823 (library binding) | ISBN 9781623108960 (pdf)
Subjects: LCSH: Bicycle motocross—Juvenile literature. | Bicycle motocross—Rules—Juvenile literature.
Classification: LCC GV1049.3 .D63 2024 (print) | LCC GV1049.3 (ebook) | DDC 796.6/22—dc23/eng/20230302
LC record available at https://lccn.loc.gov/2023008873
LC ebook record available at https://lccn.loc.gov/2023008874

Printed in China

Image Credits

Alamy: Aflo Co. Ltd. 6, 25 (br), Allan Cash Picture Library 9 (t), dpa picture alliance 28–29, John Redmond 22 (t), Kenneth Hunter 16–17, Lilyana Vynogradova 18–19, Orange Pics BV 15; AP Images: Carlos Herrera 3, Greg Baker 20–21, Martin Rickett 17, Sebastian Gollnow 25 (t); BMX Racing Group Chase Bicycles 11; Getty: Sander Koning 1, 32, Thomas Barwick 23, Zendsign 10; Shutterstock: Aleksandr Sulga 27 (white), FOTOKITA 26–27 (ramps), GROGL 12–13, Haslam Photography cover homydesign 25 (bl), KK Stock 26–27 (pink, yellow), Lilkin 31, Marek Tr 26 (purple), Sergei Bachlakov 22 (b), Tim Large 4–5; vintage.es: Vintage Everyday 9 (b)

Contents

CHAPTER 1

The Race Is On

The start gate opens. Eight BMX racers speed down the first hill. They pump the pedals on their bikes then lean into the first turn. The race is on!

READY STEADY TOKYO
3
READY STEADY TOKYO
85
Red Bull
BELL
AEON
JAPAN

Photo Finish

It's a wild, high-speed chase. The racers soar over jumps. Dirt flies up behind their spinning tires. Two racers are side by side. They sail over the final jump toward the finish line. Which one will win?

BMX stands for bicycle motocross.

CHAPTER 2

Custom Bikes

BMX racing started in the early 1970s. Riders added wide tires to bikes with small frames. The **custom**-built bikes handle well on dirt.

Freestyle BMX started shortly after racing. Bikers do flips and turns on the same ramps skateboarders use. They do tricks on curbs, rails, and stairs too.

Early BMX Racing

Early Freestyle

The Bikes

BMX bikes are small and lightweight. Most are made of **aluminum** or steel. Many riders use 20-inch (51-centimeter) wheels. The tires are wide. Some have big bumps called **knobs** that grip the dirt.

BMX bikes come in a range of sizes. The smallest are called micro minis. The biggest are Pro XXL.

PARTS OF A BMX BIKE

KNOBBY TIRES
CHAIN
(NO CHAIN GUARD)
20-INCH WHEELS

CHAPTER 3

Skills and Safety

BMX takes a lot of skill. Riders need good balance. They must have powerful leg muscles to build speed quickly.

Races are often crowded. Racers must have a sense of where other bikes are on the track. They need to be **aggressive** to make passes.

Comparing Fastest Speeds

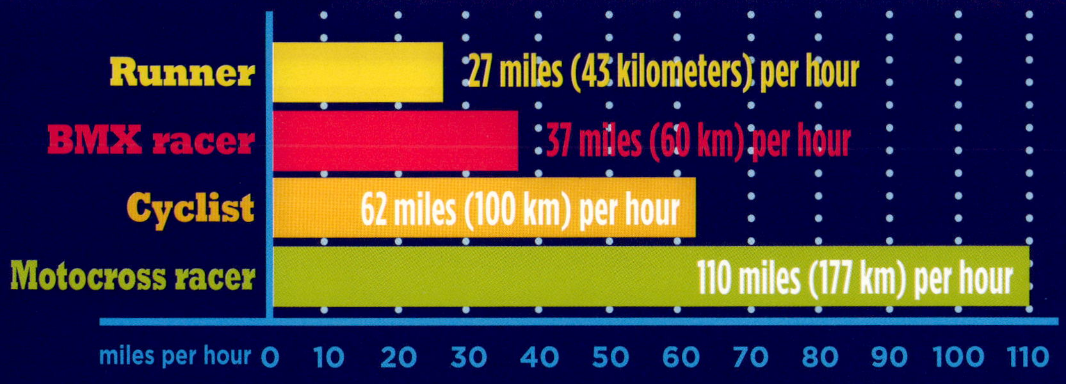

Danger!

BMX is dangerous. Racers often crash into each other. They wipe out on turns or while landing jumps. Freestyle bikers sometimes don't land a trick. Riders risk broken bones, deep cuts, and neck injuries.

BMX riders keep safety in mind. They learn how to fall safely. They keep their bikes and gear in top condition.

123
123
REDLINE
REDLINE

helmet

protects head in crash

gloves

stop sweaty hands from slipping

elbow pads

protect joints from scratches and bruises

knee pads

protect knees when falling on concrete

shin pads

protect legs from pedal pins and sharp edges

CHAPTER 4

Competitions

BMX races are fast-paced and exciting. They take place on dirt courses with lots of turns, hills, and jumps. Races are one-lap sprints to the finish.

Eight riders fight for the **holeshot**. This position leads at the first turn and sets the pace. Then it's all about speed and control. Racers must avoid crashes and stay ahead of the pack.

Track Features

berms
(angled turns)

jumps
(big hills)

rollers
(small hills)

Up, Down, and Around

Riders clear **obstacles** along the way. They skid through sharp turns. They sail over jumps. They build speed on straight sections. Multiple hills in a row test a rider's flow and skills. The fastest rider speeds across the finish line to claim victory.

Freestyle Contests

Freestyle is a popular BMX sport. Riders launch off huge ramps to do crazy flips. They ride rails on park courses. They do hops and tricks in flatland events.

Judges give riders a score from 0 to 99.9 for each run. Riders get two runs. Their score is the average of the two.

BMX riders often start very young. Riders as young as two years old can compete.

RAMPS

RAILS

FLATLAND

quarter pipe
rails

Freestyle Obstacles

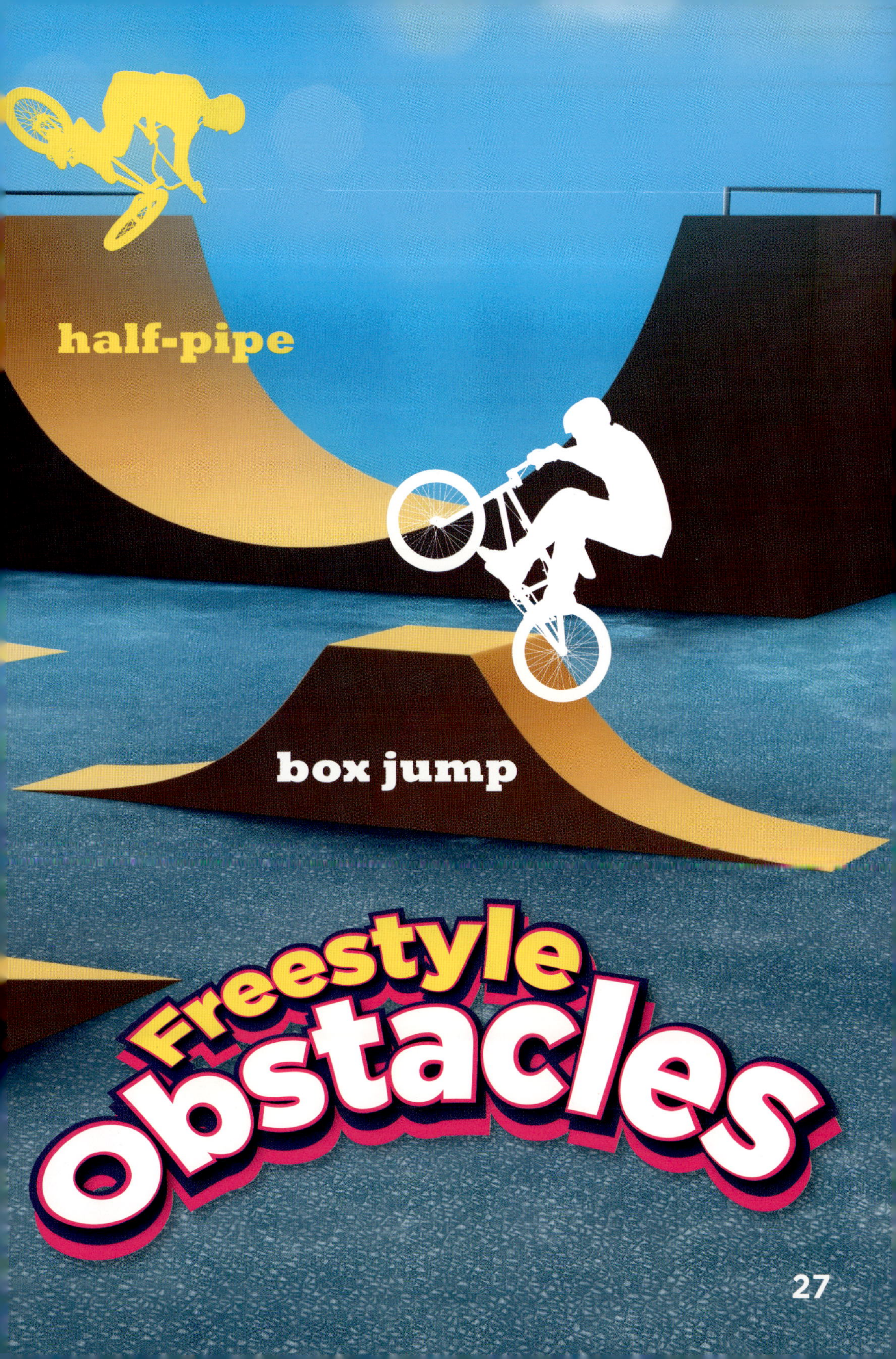

TIOGA POWERBLOCK

BMX Thrills

Freestyle BMX has many stars. Mat Hoffman, Garrett Reynolds, and Hannah Roberts have millions of fans. But you don't have to be a pro rider to enjoy freestyle. Many cities have built parks just for BMX riders. Riders practice tricks and can enjoy the sport safely.

aggressive (uh-GRES-iv)—showing a readiness to fight, argue, or attack

aluminum (uh-LOO-mih-num)—a silver-white light metallic chemical element that is easily worked

custom (KUHS-tuhm)—specially made to fit an individual's needs

freestyle (FREE-stayhl)—a competition in which the racers are able to perform tricks and skills that are judged to earn points

holeshot (HOHL-shot)—the position of the first racer who gets through the first turn in a race

knob (NOB)—a bump on a tire that makes up the tread

obstacle (OB-stuh-kuhl)—an object to go over or around

BOOKS

Amstutz, Lisa J. *The Gearhead's Guide to BMX Bikes.* North Mankato, Minn.: Spark, an imprint of Capstone, 2023.

Walker, Hubert. *BMX Racing.* Mendota Heights, Minn.: Apex, 2022.

WEBSITES

BMX Freestyle | Team USA
usacycling.org/team-usa/bmx-freestyle

The Track
www.tryusabmx.com/the-track

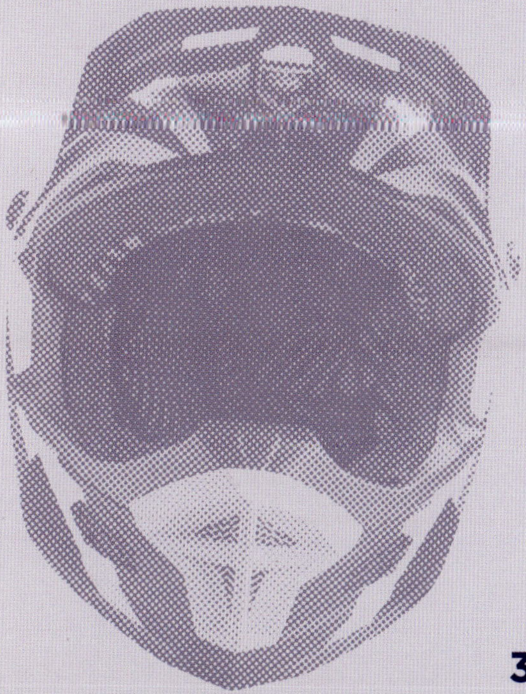

INDEX